The Family Law Doctor™ Series — BOOK 4

CAN WE STOP FIGHTING NOW?
Resolving Divorce and Post-Divorce Conflicts

By Nancy Fishman, Ph.D.

Foreword by Professor Lawrence Dubin, J.D.

The Family Law Doctor™ series includes:
Book 1: *7 Steps to a Good Divorce:
Making Smart Decisions*
(Includes *The Divorce Dictionary*)

Book 2: *Two Homes, One World:
Divorce And The Reconstituted Family*

Book 3: *Raising Happy Children After Divorce:
What To Do When Children Have Divorce Stress*

Book 4: *Can We Stop Fighting Now?:
Resolving Divorce And Post-Divorce Conflicts*

The Divorce Client's Workbook: *A Companion to
7 Steps to a Good Divorce: Making Smart Decisions*

PUBLISHED BY MOMENTUM BOOKS, LLC

117 West Third Street | Royal Oak, Michigan 48067

www.momentumbooks.com

ISBN: 978-1-879094-90-1

LCCN: 2010938053

This book is dedicated to my daughter,
Beth Anstandig Killough, for teaching me
patience and perseverance.

CAN WE STOP FIGHTING NOW?
Resolving Divorce and Post-Divorce Conflicts

CHAPTER 5:

SUMMARY AND TAKEAWAYS

FOREWORD

Professor Larry Dubin, J.D.
University of Detroit Mercy School of Law

It seems logical that angry spouses will become even angrier during a divorce. After all, there is more to fight over once legal proceedings are initiated. During a divorce action, property has to be divided, financial arrangements have to be made for child support and possible alimony, and decisions about future child issues (custody, visitation, etc.) must be determined.

Decades ago, lawyers viewed the anger of their divorce clients as fuel to justify high fees and many court appearances to decide these delicate family issues. The lawyer's perspective was that the legal dismantling of a marriage was similar to the dissolution of a business. The emotional trauma suffered by the divorce litigants and their children was considered collateral damage in the same way innocent civilians are unfortunately wounded or killed during a war.

Thankfully, enlightenment has finally occurred due in large part to many lawyers, judges, and psychologists who recognized that divorce does not have to be made more difficult for couples or their children by lawyers who sometimes use their advocacy to create more contentiousness and more pain. As Bob Dylan observed, "The times, they are a-changing."

Can We Stop Fighting Now? Resolving Divorce and Post-Divorce Conflicts sets forth more humane and reasonable ways for people to approach the process of divorce. Instead of the parties constantly fighting, an alternative method is presented for working out disputes. Rather than children suffering permanent psychological damage during and after the divorce of their parents, strategies are offered to help their parents remain a consistently loving and unified presence in their lives.

Does what this book offers sound too good to be true? Are the recommendations too idealistic and unrealistic for people seeking divorce as a final option to terminate their marriage? I think not. For those who want to stay angry and maintain a "win at all costs" attitude, the legal system is more than ready to meet their needs. For the more enlightened couples who want to avoid the negative consequences of a messy divorce, this book offers many practical suggestions for ways to avoid the harsh results that often flow from a highly contested divorce action.

As a law professor who served eight years as a Michigan Supreme Court appointee to the Michigan Attorney Grievance Commission (the entity that prosecutes lawyers for acts of misconduct), I have read many grievances over the years from divorce clients who were angry at their lawyers after the divorce—and with some justification. They felt their lawyers were insensitive to their emotional pain during the legal battles that occurred leading up to the divorce or during post-divorce matters. In reading these grievances, I asked myself, when will the people who run the legal system (judges, lawyers, Friend of the Court personnel, etc.) finally realize that change is desperately needed?

This book is a recipe for that change. It is a prescription for getting as healthy a divorce as possible as well as forming a template to deal with post-divorce issues that may arise. Now there is a choice. Couples can either go the traditional route of fighting over many issues and paying in extra dollars and emotional pain, or they can take the information offered in this book and seek a non-confrontational divorce that not only meets their emotional needs, but puts the best interests of their children first.

Professor Larry Dubin
University of Detroit Mercy School of Law,
former Chair of the Michigan Attorney
Grievance Commission

There are times in everyone's life when something constructive is born from adversity ... when things seem so bad that you've got to grab your fate by the shoulders and shake it.
—Anonymous

Out of conflict comes change.
—Rollo May, Ph.D.

People wish to be settled; only as far as they are unsettled is there any hope for them.
—Ralph Waldo Emerson

Difficulties are meant to rouse, not discourage. The human spirit is to grow by conflict.
—William Ellery Channing

INTRODUCTION

The fight for territory and resources is as old as the cave. Add the drive for power and we have a classic conflict from the sandbox to the sandlot, from Malaysia to the Middle East, from island to island, and from one divorce court to the next.

I recall only one argument my parents had as I was growing up. As a naval officer during World War II, my father saw six invasions from a tanker. After that, he never wanted to fight or take a cruise for the rest of his life. One very hot summer, my father wanted to install central air conditioning for my mother, who was bedridden with cancer. She didn't want to spend the money. I heard them raise their voices to each other! He won the battle, and five minutes later she was on the phone with her sister, giddy with excitement.

I was in the seventh grade when I witnessed a domestic fight for the first time at my girlfriend's house. Her parents fought conspicuously and without shame—calling each other names and slinging accusations—over how much money to give their daughter for a pair of shoes. The fighting was a strange, yet compelling phenomenon for me. It made me terribly uncomfortable and, at the same time, curious. What was all that screaming about? Surely not twenty bucks for a pair of shoes.

As my own world grew, I realized that conflict came in all sizes, shapes, and colors. My curiosity also grew—

I began to study the ways conflicts are resolved.

Much later, while living on a northern Caribbean island shared by two separate nations, I asked the question: How have these two unique cultures shared such a small space so successfully for so many years? It turns out they actually had a shared experience which drew them together.

Once upon a time, the original island inhabitants were all members of the Arawak tribe. (Why, then, was the sea surrounding the islands not called the Arawak Sea?) As the story goes, the Arawaks were a very peaceful people, community-minded with great negotiating skills. They worked together to compile and share resources. Their home became known as the "friendly island."

Eventually, the Arawaks had visitors, called the Caribes, from another island off the coast of South America. The Caribes were a rather rough bunch. Conflict was an everyday part of their lives. When they arrived on the friendly island, they knew they were in paradise. It was a land of plenty, and they helped themselves to everything. You can imagine how intrigued they were with the Arawaks, who were so friendly and generous. Well, the Caribes liked the Arawaks so much that they ate most of them!

Thankfully, there are many others ways to negotiate for territory and resources. Whether you are trading dump trucks in a sandbox, land for peace in the Middle East, or vying for more parenting time during a divorce, you must be able to express your needs and convince others to help you meet them.

Divorce, by its very nature, requires the division of territory and resources. Divorce attorneys can be helpful in negotiating an equitable settlement, but the final decree never comes with a guarantee of satisfaction, nor a manual for solving future disputes. When children are involved, the goal should be to create a "friendly island"—a conflict-free environment so the children can grow and thrive without the worries of the adult world.

How children survive a family's divorce is directly correlated to the way their parents handle the divorce, manage their differences, and resolve their conflicts. After divorce, the co-parenting relationship is the single most important contributing factor to children's happiness.

This book is written to give divorcing and post-divorce parties practical ways of settling arguments that actually enhance the relationship, build a new trust, and preserve a positive co-parenting bond.

First, you will discover why certain conversations seem impossible to have—then you will learn how to have them with success. I have also chosen several of the most-frequently reported arguments and have included real-life examples of how people have managed to screw them up. After each example, I have provided a more preferred way of having the conversation so it will become productive and satisfying to both parents.

Hopefully, you will realize the benefits of having a better way to solve differences. When you are secure with your method of dispute resolution, you will trust the plan first and then build a new trust with your co-parent.

Whether you want to make a change in child support or parenting time, or you want to discuss your children's activities or attitudes, you must create a "friendly island" with your co-parent to accomplish your goals for the benefit of your children. Teach them to play well in the sandbox. Show them that anything is possible when peace for their sake is the priority.

—*Dr. Nancy Fishman, October 2010*

CHAPTER 1

THE DIVORCE WAR ZONE
The Judges and Attorneys Speak
Having Conversations Without Fighting
Familiar Conversations
Summary and Takeaways

THE DIVORCE WAR ZONE

Divorce is an emotionally charged experience that comes at a time when trust has broken down to a significant degree in a relationship. Hopes and dreams are shattered, and the weight of disappointment becomes a seemingly impossible burden to shoulder.

When divorce happens between childless parties, all disputes are resolved one way or another during the divorce process. At the end of the process, the marriage is over, and parties without children never need to see or speak to each other again.

However, when divorce happens for couples with children, the marriage may be over, but a co-parenting relationship needs to continue, leaving open the potential for future disputes. Typical feelings—like anger, sadness, and fear—compound the difficulty in trying to communicate about family and parenting issues. There are always decisions to make and conflicts to resolve. With emotions heightened, you and your former spouse may find yourselves reverting to old, ineffective habits of communicating. Some people argue openly, while others find quieter, safer means of expressing their disagreements.

In truth, no two people are in tune with everything. Divorce is a likely arena for doing battle about current points of contention, as well as unresolved issues from the past—the ones you swept under the carpet to keep the peace or didn't know how else to resolve.

Divorce court could have been a giant war zone over the emotional garbage you collected for years. At the end of the divorce, when the gavel hit the wood, you and your former spouse may have found yourselves in worse shape than at any time during your marriage. During your divorce, you negotiated an asset and liability settlement, you created a parenting time plan, but did you agree on a way to settle arguments after the divorce? You fought during your marriage; you battled during your divorce. Why should you believe you could do better now? Furthermore, why should you even try?

The most important reason to stop fighting now is to provide a conflict-free zone for your children.

Children need to love and be loved by both parents without fear of hurting or disappointing their parents. They need to be able to grow up unfettered by the complications of adult relationships. They need to be free of worry that they have done something to cause the strife between their parents. Children who grow up in a family that doesn't handle conflict well are at greater risk to develop a multitude of symptoms associated with anxiety and depression. While it is unrealistic to imagine life without any conflicts, parents bear a huge responsibility for providing children with opportunities to learn how to manage conflicts. Even divorced parents can model good conflict resolution.

Believe it or not, some of the best parenting

partners are divorced parents. The ending of your marriage partnership does not prevent you from being great partners in parenting. For some of you, this concept may seem completely alien, especially if you experienced a rather messy divorce. However, you will be linked to your child's other parent forever. Whatever happens to your children, whether it be a great moment in life or the worst imaginable nightmare, only one other person in the entire world will feel exactly the way you do—the other parent. This is a rare connection that is advisable to preserve.

You may feel a little vulnerable with the other parent sharing both child-rearing responsibilities and thrills, but there are many benefits in being able to coordinate efforts. Your children are entitled to have two parents who love them and want to work together to help them thrive, who are there to catch them when they fall, and to enjoy the precious moments in life as well.

Working together as parenting partners first begins with the commitment to put your children's best interests before your own feelings. Initially this may require some tongue-holding, constant compromise, and a lot of patience. But once you have experienced some success in co-parenting, you will want to be "Parents of the Year." When your children are grown and reflect upon their childhood, you hope they will say that you and their other parent were always there for them together.

The commitment to resolve conflicts amicably is challenging! Two issues that cause the most conflict and are disputed most frequently between divorced co-parents are finances and parenting time. Broadly speaking, the divorce settlement covers money, custody, and child-rearing responsibilities. Realistically, though, changes occur throughout the span of the children's growing-up years—often necessitating adjustments to the original agreement.

A dispute resolution clause is often absent from the written divorce settlement, so once the divorce is over, you have no roadmap to guide you through your arguments. Without a plan, your smallest spats can become full-blown battles. This never promotes a good co-parenting relationship and is absolutely destructive for everyone in the family.

I highly suggest that a dispute resolution plan be in place for the times when you just cannot agree. Dispute resolution requires the willingness of you and your former spouse to engage in negotiations about touchy topics until you come to a conclusion with which you both can live. The conclusions may not be ideal for either of you, but they must be workable and durable.

Following are a few methods of resolving post-divorce disputes:

- The most extreme measure of dispute resolution between co-parents is to appear before the court.

This is the least preferable option because the judge does not know the intricacies of your family and may intervene in ways less acceptable to both of you. It is also costly, contentious, and does not promote the confidence, motivation, nor the feelings of success needed for conflict resolution on future issues.

- A parenting coordinator is sometimes appointed by the court either through the Friend of the Court or by agreement of the parties to help resolve conflicts and encourage positive decision-making.

- Each judge has at least one referee and a Friend of the Court counselor assigned to him or her. Sometimes the judge may ask the referee to settle disputes between co-parents.

- A Friend of the Court counselor employed by the county is assigned to your family. Parties can call the Friend of the Court counselor directly to assist in conflict resolution.

- If your divorce settlement has a post-divorce dispute resolution clause, you may choose to exercise that plan. The clause usually names a neutral professional whom you, your former spouse, and your attorneys had agreed at the finalization of the divorce would be the "go-to" person if you hit a snag post-divorce. Your neutral "go-to" may be a therapist, counselor, mediator, or divorce coach. Use your resources before you allow your co-parenting relationship to deteriorate.

- In the end, it is always advisable to talk between yourselves. Express your ideas and listen to each other. Look for common ground. You may actually devise a compromise that works for both of you and is in the best interests of your family. If you are able to resolve your conflicts together without assistance, your successes will become building blocks for future experiences.

Remember: The importance of "family" is always magnified and accentuated for children of divorce. Resolving conflict is part of every family's life. Children tend to blame themselves for whatever goes wrong between parents. If you do not demonstrate civility when resolving disputes, your children will blame themselves! In order to thrive, they need to see their parents joining forces as successful co-parents devoted to the family. Be good role models for your children. Show them that conflict is not frightening and can be overcome with reason and respect. Your personal feelings are not as important as your children's needs.

Now, more than ever, I am convinced that the way people resolve their differences makes the greatest impact on their relationships, the emotional health of their children, and the success of their families.

CHAPTER 2

THE JUDGES AND ATTORNEYS SPEAK

Family law judges and attorneys have a unique perspective on families of divorce because they witness the stress that occurs between divorcing parties. Even after a divorce is final, parties sometimes return to the legal arena to make changes in their divorce agreements and to ask the court for a variety of interventions. Family law judges and attorneys are constantly observing the effects of divorce on children, especially when parties return to court post-divorce to resolve ongoing conflicts.

I invited several family law judges and attorneys with whom I have personally worked to address the affects of conflict on children. I hope you will appreciate their advice as much as I do and find some suggestions that will resonate with you.

I posed the following question to the judges and attorneys:

What advice would you give to divorcing parties with children?

Following are the responses they shared, appearing in alphabetical order.

From The Honorable Judge:
JAMES M. ALEXANDER, J.D.

Oakland County Family Court
1200 North Telegraph Road
Pontiac, MI 48341

Parents need to understand that the court looks at the "best interests of the children," not the best interests of the parents. Parents must also do that. Children are not pawns, nor property to be used to gain an advantage. While the divorce ends the spousal relationship, it maintains the parent relationship. This is a lifetime commitment, and the actions taken during and after the divorce will have lasting consequences. Remember, at some point your child will walk down the aisle … you want them to want you to be there with them.

From Attorney:
LORI BECKER, J.D., M.B.A.

Becker Law Firm
33 Bloomfield Hills Parkway, Suite 270
Bloomfield Hills, MI 48304
p: (248) 885-8660 | **e:** lbecker@beckerlegalgroup.com
w: www.beckerlegalgroup.com

The most important decision a divorcing couple can make is choosing *how* they divorce. Once the decision to divorce is made, the primary focus is often on getting to the finish line. But in between, a family's structure and stability is at stake. Finalizing a divorce powered by short-term anger prevents parents from creating long-term family goals. Highly contentious, drawn-out divorce can have a devastating effect on children. But what about the children's children? Divorces impact generations. How a child experiences the process can affect how that child raises his or her own family.

Redirecting a couple in the early stages of divorce to focus on the best interests of the children is crucial. This key component of divorce is sorely missing from the litigation process and the way most people think about divorce. Divorcing couples must take the time to explore their options, such as the collaborative process, mediation, or other forms of alternative dispute resolution, and choose a process that helps restructure their family in the most productive manner.

From Attorney:
JUDITH BLUMENO, J.D.

32400 Telegraph Road, Suite 104
Bingham Farms, MI 48025
p: (248) 593-9090 | **e:** jblumeno@judithblumeno.com
w: www.judithblumeno.com

I advise my clients that both parents are and always will be the children's only parents. No matter what each party thinks of the other, they have to put aside their hurt, anger, hard feelings, and all negativity and be able to work together for the good of their children. They are each equally entitled to the love and respect of their children. Each parent should respect the rules in the other parent's home so there can be consistency in the children's lives.

Because these parties have children, there will be many occasions when they both will be in the same place at the same time—for graduations, birthdays, weddings, births of grandchildren, and other important events in their children's lives. They need to be civil to each other.

I also advise them not to discuss issues regarding divorce; these are adult issues. The parties have to be sure not to disparage or make negative remarks about the other parent when the children are present. Children are entitled to as much time with each parent as is possible under the circumstances of the divorce.

From Attorney:
RONALD M. BOOKHOLDER, J.D.

1111 West Long Lake Road, Suite 201
Troy, Michigan 48090
p: (248) 641-0100 | **e:** bookholder@aol.com
w: www.bookholderlaw.com

I encourage parents to maintain civility with their spouse for the benefit of their children. I suggest the parents see a therapist together and discuss how, when, and what to tell their children. The parties should reinforce that their children will have two homes, as Mom and Dad are going to be living separately after the divorce, and the children will have two homes in which they are loved by both parents. I suggest that parents emphasize to their children that they are not responsible for the divorce. I recommend the parents tell the children's teachers and social workers about the divorce and request that they be notified of any new issues their children are having in school.

I remind the parents that children are very perceptive and recognize the parents' feelings toward each other. I caution the parents that the children should not discover their parents are divorcing from others. Parents should remember their children pick up on body language and are going to be affected by the uncertainty of divorce. The effects of conflict between parents negatively impacts children. I tell parents that it is extremely hurtful to children to have one parent make negative and disparaging comments about the other parent. I remind parents their actions affect their children and to remember that as hard as the divorce is on them, it is very difficult for their children to accept. How you handle yourself in a divorce will affect your children. I caution parents to be alert to the effects of divorce on the children, and to consider engaging a child therapist to assist the children throughout the divorce. Most importantly, I remind the parents that for children to be emotionally healthy they need both parents.

The information above I primarily give to parents with minor children. However, I advise parents that divorce impacts adult children, too. Maintaining civility and not disparaging the other parent is important to enable the parents of minor and adult children to be at significant events in their children's and grandchildren's lives without the children having to walk on eggshells, worrying that one or both parents will act inappropriately and embarrass the children and themselves, spoiling the occasion for everyone.

From Attorney:
CAROL F. BREITMEYER, J.D.

Hickey, Cianciolo, Fishman & Finn, PC
211 West Fort Street, Suite 615
Detroit, Michigan 48226
p: (313) 962-4600 | **e:** cfb@hclawyers.com
w: www.hclawyers.com

In cases with minor children, potential clients are somewhat surprised when I explain in the initial interview that if a custody/parenting time matter proceeds to trial, I feel that I have failed at my job. Family matters need thoughtful, carefully fashioned, and timely resolution. Those words do not necessarily describe a contested custody matter. I do my best to move parties away from the notion of "sole physical custody." We talk instead about parenting time, about collaboration, and about crafting solutions, not causing problems.

In my experience, the process of divorce frequently crystallizes the pre-filing family dynamic. Sometimes we can capitalize on this. I ask my parties to be at their best, hard as it is, to make an effort to "practice" for post-judgment. I ask them to step up to the task, not sink to the lowest levels, tempting as that may be. One of the attorney's jobs, in my view, is to keep sight of the bigger picture and remind a client of the long-range goals, even if they see it as a short-term "weakness."

Long-term marriages present the most complicated divorce scenarios. The deep interconnections, even in toxic relationships, make for a remarkably painful and poignant transition. I tell the client this and I virtually always insist on counseling: marital, exit, individual—any of it helps.

There are always exceptions to the foregoing; some battles genuinely need to be waged. But the majority of clients will be responsive to good stewardship, and I firmly believe it is our duty to guide our clients in this positive fashion.

I tend to be positive, but I strive to provide a realistic outlook. I encourage the client to read about the issues they will face. The transition from married to single, especially for those with children and/or long-term marriages, is an arduous process. As family attorneys, we are the stewards of this transition, and our task is not easy if it is done properly. Making a war where none need be violates our mutual goal of our work as attorneys in family law.

From Attorney:
Henry S. Gornbein, J.D.

40900 Woodward Avenue, Suite 111
Bloomfield Hills, MI 48304
p: (248) 594-3444
e: hgornbein@familylawofmichigan.com
w: www.familylawofmichigan.com

In my many years of specializing in family law, I have found the greatest disservice parents can do to their children is to put them in the middle of divorce. I find that needless custody battles harm everyone, but especially children.

Too often parents forget about what is best for their children in their anger and desire to punish each other. Step back. Try to communicate with each other and not through your children. Do not use your children as pawns. Make your children feel loved, and make it clear to them that they have no responsibility with regard to the fact that you, the adults, have decided to end your marriage. Even though your marriage is over, you will be parents for the rest of your lives. Do not speak negatively about the other parent in front of the children. This includes not only words, but also gestures. Remember that once something is said, it is very difficult to take it back. Try to make your children feel as comfortable and loved as possible. Don't try to buy the children or bribe them. Carry out normal routines with your children, whether you have them for half the time, or most of the time. Do things you normally do. Don't become a Disneyland dad or mom. Don't try to outbid the other parent. Remember that children are very manipulative, and even in an intact marriage, children will play one parent against the other.

In a divorce, children want to be able to share events long after the divorce is over. This means your children should feel free to love each one of you. You should be able to go to parent/teacher conferences, school plays, dance recitals, sporting events, and be able to sit, if not next to each other, at least in close proximity so your children feel both of you are supporting them. You want to be able to be at life events such as confirmations, graduations, bar mitzvahs, weddings, and other significant events, where everyone can be as comfortable as possible. Sometimes this is difficult, but these goals are worth achieving.

From The Honorable Judge:
LINDA S. HALLMARK, J.D.

Oakland County Family Court
1200 North Telegraph Road
Pontiac, MI 48341

Parents are life partners, even following a divorce. As
we advise parents during our SMILE (Start Making
It Liveable for Everyone) program, conflict between
parents can have disastrous consequences for children.
Children exposed to long-term parental conflict
frequently suffer physical and/or emotional harm.
Our goal for a healthy society is to reduce conflict in
children's lives and allow them to thrive. We strongly
encourage those who are struggling with conflict to
get assistance from one of our excellent community
resources. We wish you and your children a bright
and happy future.

From Attorney:
ADA SNYDER KERWIN, J.D., M.S.W.

Clark Hill, PLLC
151 South Old Woodward Avenue, Suite 200
Birmingham, MI 48009
p: (248) 988-5886 | **e:** akerwin@clarkhill.com
w: www.clarkhill.com

A parent going through a divorce needs to distinguish between their own needs and the children's needs. For example, the parent might believe a strict 50/50 parenting plan is important for their child when, in reality, the need for that plan is really the parent's need.

Most children need both parents to be involved and available but are not concerned about parenting time being strictly equal. In order to construct a parenting plan that addresses the unique needs of a particular family, consulting with an experienced professional is extremely helpful. An experienced professional, whether a family law attorney and/or a psychotherapist who specializes in children and families, will help the parents avoid some of the common parenting plan pitfalls as well as guide the parents in finding a workable parenting plan that's in the best interests of their children. There are no "cookie cutter" families. Therefore, there are no "cookie cutter" parenting plans.

Always apply the Golden Rule. Treat your divorcing spouse as you want to be treated, without expecting anything in return. By doing so, you will generate goodwill and optimize the opportunity to be treated well by the other parent.

From Attorney:
PAUL S. KOWAL, J.D.

Attorneys and Counselors at Law
8152 Twenty-Five Mile Road, Suite B-1
Shelby Township, MI 48316
p: (586) 781-9190 | **e:** pskowal@pflcenter.com
w: www.gregoryfilar.biz

The best advice I can give to divorcing parents is not to involve their children in adult matters. Often a divorcing parent feels compelled to tell the children "the truth" of why the parties are divorcing. Regardless of the parent's motivation for discussing adult topics with the children, it is wrong. A child lacks the life skills necessary to cope with the information, whether the child is a tot or a teenager.

We have all been taught to respect the Office of the President of the United States, even if we do not respect the person occupying that office. I would advise each parent to respect the "Office of Mom and Dad." Children have been taught since birth to love both of their parents equally and unconditionally. How can we switch horses midstream and now teach them that parents should be loved conditionally? Parents should never say an unkind word about each other when their children are present, with an emphasis on present. If the children are in the same vicinity as you are, they will hear you even when you are sure they are not listening. The best thing you can do for your children is to treat their mother or father well, love them if you can, and at least be respectful.

Finally, if you have the means, it would not hurt for the parents to obtain counseling for their children. The children need to be heard by someone impartial. If you cannot afford a counselor, many schools and churches offer programs for children of divorce that can be helpful.

From Attorney:
SUSAN E. PALETZ, J.D.

Paletz Law Firm, PC
32400 Telegraph Road, Suite 104
Bingham Farms, MI 48025
p: (248) 203-6800 | **e:** info@paletzlaw.com
w: www.Paletzlaw.com

One of the most important things parties going through a divorce should strongly consider is to refrain from introducing their children to a third party during the divorce proceeding and even for several months after the divorce is final. It is always surprising to me when a parent feels it is appropriate and acceptable to introduce children to a person they have a relationship with, even though they have recently filed for divorce or are in the divorce process. Yet, over the years I have encountered this behavior by both mothers and fathers.

Not surprisingly, this often heightens the level of animosity between the parents and adds to the emotional stress in a situation that is already difficult. In addition, this is a time when children need to have the full attention of their parents. Introduction of a third party often creates a significant amount of stress for the child.

Although it seems that this advice is common sense, there are many parents who think that as long as they are getting divorced, it is OK for the children to be introduced to a third party. The parents need to think about what is going on from the children's perspective.

The children are going through major changes, including the loss of the family unit and sometimes a perceived loss of a parent. Therefore, the parents need to focus on the needs of the child and not on another party during parenting time.

From Attorney:
ALISA A. PESKIN-SHEPERD, J.D.

40900 Woodward Avenue, Suite 111
Bloomfield Hills, MI 48304
p: (248) 594-3444 | **e:** aps@familylaw.com
w: www.familylawofmichigan.com

Recognize your children's needs and put them before your own when making tough decisions, whether the decision involves parenting time, support, or property settlement. No matter how you feel about your spouse, take a breath and ask yourself: "Is this in my child's best interest, or am I doing this to hurt or to compete with my spouse?"

Your children are going to love both of you because you are their parents.

What your children want or need during early or elementary school years will be very different from their needs and desires (and attitudes) when they are in middle school and high school. Be willing to be flexible for your children in terms of your parenting time and even in financial situations to your ability. Even if you do not have much flexibility in the parenting time plan of your final divorce judgment, you and the other parent can work together and agree to make changes on your own.

Use the court as your last resort. There are many alternative ways to resolve a dispute you are having with the other parent. Be willing to sit down with the other parent, with your attorneys or alone, or with the assistance of a neutral third party, such as a mediator, facilitator, or co-parenting coordinator trained in this area of family law. This could be a mental health professional, an attorney, or clergy from your religious institution. As much as possible, resolve disagreements with the other parent outside of court. You know your children much better than any judge. The judge, the courtroom, and the legal system frequently promote anxiety in parents. As a result, a parent may say something in court that they never would have said in a less litigious and anxiety-provoking environment. But once the words are out, you can't take them back. The more that you and the children's other parent can work out together, outside of court, with the best interests of your children at the forefront of your mind, the more satisfied you and your children will feel.

Sometimes you have to be the parent who takes the high road, which sometimes may feel like all the time to you, but your satisfaction will be greater.

There are many large and small details that arise as you and your spouse co-parent your children, everything from participation in extracurricular activities to a refusal by the other parent to receive any e-mail from you unless it is sent from a particular e-mail account. Just as parents often "pick their battles" with their children, so too will you find this to be true, and in your child's best interest, with regard to many day-to-day co-parenting details. Your former spouse's request for a different e-mail carrier may bother you and seem completely unreasonable, but what will it take for you to open up a free e-mail account with another provider? Probably not much. Rather than engaging your former spouse in a battle over a seemingly unreasonable request, you eliminated a conflict by taking the high road. If communication has been an issue, the other parent cannot now complain that he or she is not receiving e-mail, which may not have reached you previously if it had been considered spam or junk mail.

There may be an extracurricular activity that your child wants to participate in, but you know that if you open the door to ask the other parent to share the cost, it will create tension and animosity with your former spouse. Can you afford the activity on your own? Is it worth making an unstable co-parenting relationship even more difficult? These are questions you have to ask yourself.

But without doubt, when you take the high road instead of digging your heels in based on principle, you will come out feeling better on the other side, and your child will not be exposed to conflict between his or her parents. Can you think of a time when this isn't in your child's best interest?

From Attorney:
RANDALL B. PITLER, J.D.

Pitler Family Law & Mediation, PC
25892 Woodward Avenue
Royal Oak, MI 48067
p: (248) 584-0400 | **e:** rpitler@pitlerlaw.com
w: www.amicabledivorce.com

Once couples make the difficult decision to divorce, I advise them to begin planning for their lives post-divorce, both emotionally and financially. Financial planning includes preparing budgets with their post-divorce income and expenses and meeting with a financial planner to adjust their retirement goals.

Most importantly, they need to begin preparing for a lifetime of co-parenting. Many divorcing parents assume their responsibilities as parents begin and end during their parenting time window or that they will be able to parent during their own parenting time window without any input from the other spouse. They fail to anticipate how much communication is necessary to co-parent successfully.

Logistically, parents will need to rely on each other and continue to work as a team on minor issues, such as making sure homework is completed and getting children to their extracurricular activities on time. Bigger issues, such as completing college student loan applications, also require teamwork.

Nowadays, it is critical that parents agree on and enforce consistent computer and cell phone usage limits to avoid allowing the children to set their own boundaries, making parental oversight nearly impossible.

Further, many divorcing parents fail to recognize that co-parenting does not end at high school graduation. Parents must continue to give advice, plus emotional and financial support, to their children forever. They will also attend certain life events together, such as weddings or the birth of grandchildren. Co-parenting is not easy, but putting the children first from the outset will make the process less difficult.

From Attorney:
B. ANDREW RIFKIN, J.D.

The Law Firm of John F. Schaefer
380 North Old Woodward Avenue, Suite 320
Birmingham, MI 48009
p: (248) 642-6655 | **e:** bar@lfjfs.com
w: www.lfjfs.com

Do whatever it takes to avoid a contested custody trial or hearing involving your children. The worst parenting schedule in the world is better than a contested custody trial or hearing. Contested parenting and custody issues decided by a referee or judge never result in decisions as good as the ones that could have been reached by the parents themselves. That's because no one knows the children better than the parents do. A referee or judge simply does not have the time or expertise to get to know you, your children, and your unique circumstances well enough to reach a decision that is appropriate for your particular situation and in the best interests of your children. Left to the judge, the process of reaching that decision inevitably destroys any remaining chance of a civil relationship between the parents, causing the children to suffer even more. Beyond the fact that litigated decisions involving children rarely are appropriate to the family's unique circumstances, litigated custody trials or hearings usually lead to more contested trials and hearings, either because the "losing" parent continually tries to upset the unfavorable result, or because the result is insufficient to address all the needs of the parents and the children. Inevitably, litigating parents spend far more money, time, and emotional energy than do parents who try to negotiate an effective resolution; at the same time, these litigating parents end up with a result that is much worse. Parents would be far better served by investing their time, energy, and money with their attorneys and a qualified mediator and/or a trained parenting coordinator. These professionals can assist the parents in establishing a long-term forum and mechanism to work out these difficult and ongoing issues, leading to solutions that ultimately are effective not only at the time the case is resolved, but also as the children—and their needs and schedules—grow and change.

From Attorney:
ABBIE SHUMAN, J.D.

23656 Hunters Lane
Southfield, MI 48033
p: (248)-356-4963 | **e:** abbie123@aol.com

As an attorney appointed by the court to represent the interests of the children in divorce and custody cases, I have the following advice for divorcing and divorced parents: Take the money that you plan to spend on attorneys to contest who gets the coffee maker and the dog and put it into an account (joint or with someone you agree on) for your children's college education. You will be amazed at how fast it adds up, and neither parent will ever feel that it was a waste of funds—which inevitably one party or the other ends up feeling.

Again—take the funds that you might otherwise expend on lawyers and go to mediation instead. It is cheaper, and cuts the costs of divorce considerably. More importantly, mediation often resolves issues that were thought to be impossible to agree upon.

Assume that you are never going to be really divorced from your spouse. As long as you have children in common, you are linked until you die. So accept that whatever you did not like about your spouse is not going away, and move on with your life.

Never share your feelings about your ex-spouse with your children. It only comes back to haunt you.

From Attorney:
DANIELLE A. SMITH, J.D.

Michigan Divorce Options
33 Bloomfield Hills Parkway, Suite 230
Bloomfield Hills, MI 48304
p: (248) 519-2323
e: dsmith@michigandivorceoptions.com
w: www.michigandivorceoptions.com

Why does the legal system take parents, who were partners in the most intimate human relationship, and turn them into adversaries? It makes no sense.

Nonetheless, Michigan divorce laws favor both parents having healthy relationships with their children, and there is a strong presumption for joint custody in every divorce or custody matter. How does the adversarial nature of divorce match the parents' values? Unfortunately, all too often it does not.

Parties going through divorce need to be assured that the interaction children have and will have with both parents after the divorce is what is most important. Parents must be encouraged, despite their differences, to learn how to work together for their children's future health, stability, and success, and they need reassurance that they can do it.

Unfortunately, divorce often creates an emotional atmosphere of mistrust between the parents, resulting in hurt, anger, and sometimes revenge. Vital for parents going through divorce is the fact that their children need both of them. Fighting over children harms the children, not the other spouse. It is critical to remember and remind the parents that during a divorce neither parent is herself or himself.

Parents have a lot of fears when they become divorced. They fear loss of the family, their parental role, and time with their children. They fear the children will favor and love the other parent more. They fear the other parent will try to buy the children's affection, time, and love with lavish monetary objects. They fear there will never be enough money to raise the children as was previously planned during the marriage. Spouses going through divorce must understand the other parent has these same fears.

Encouraging divorcing parents to recognize that the children naturally love and need both of them is crucial. Restructuring the family after divorce is much better served through alternative dispute resolution processes, such as the collaborative process or mediation. These processes encourage parents to protect their children from the trauma of a full-blown adversarial litigated divorce with subpoenas, interrogatories, depositions, and unknown third parties making decisions for them. After all the fighting and mudslinging, the attorneys are the financial winners, the court just doesn't care, each of the parents is an emotional loser, and their children are damaged without any voice in the process.

From Attorney:
DANIEL VICTOR, J.D.

Law Firm of Victor and Victor, PLLC
100 West Long Lake Road, Suite 250
Bloomfield Hills, MI 48304
p: (248) 646-7177
e: danny@victorandvictorlaw.com
w: www.victorandvictorlaw.com

My advice to parents going through a divorce consists of three key points:

• Parents must remember to view, perceive, and frame the divorce process as part of the continuum that makes up the entire timeline of the family's history: past, present, and future. A divorce affects the family, not just the parents. In time, the members of the family unit—though reshaped after the divorce—should be able to place the dissolution of the marriage in context within the larger picture of the life of each family member.

• Adults solve problems differently than children. Parents often view divorce as a solution to a troubled marriage—and therefore a solution to a problem. Viewing divorce in this context alone is common for adults, but makes little sense to children, who are not engaged in the same problem-solving endeavor as their parents. To the contrary, the parents' solution—the divorce—actually causes a problem for the children that the children did not have before. Divorcing parents must recognize that while solving one adult problem, they must also be dedicated to solving an entirely different problem for their children.

• Divorcing parents are faced with perhaps the most unnatural challenge a human being must face. The challenge is to teach someone you love (your child) to love someone you no longer love (your former spouse). Teaching the most precious person in your life to love someone you do not love is contrary to human nature, yet it is essential for a child's mental and emotional health. Since there is no easy solution to this dilemma, my advice is that parents must be vigilantly conscious of their responsibility to encourage a positive, healthy, and loving relationship between their child and their child's other parent, in spite of their own actual adult feelings.

From Attorney:
RICHARD VICTOR, J.D.

Law Firm of Victor and Victor, PLLC
100 West Long Lake Road, Suite 250
Bloomfield Hills, MI 48304
p: (248) 646-7177 | **e:** rsvlaw@aol.com
w: www.victorandvictorlaw.com

Adult decisions come with adult responsibilities. Getting married, committing to have children, and deciding to separate and divorce are all adult decisions. When parents divorce, their adult decision will impact not only their future, but also the future of their children and most probably their children's children. Children are not consulted nor part of the adult process to divorce. But, the impact the divorce will have in their lives can be similar to being an innocent victim of a "drive-by shooting." They find that they live with the result of being in a set of circumstances over which they had no control but will impact them forever.

Parents must realize that children are not property, nor are they commodities to be traded as part of the divorce process. They may be little people, but they have unique feelings and needs. Most children will put themselves second to what they believe their parent wants. They usually tell parents things they think parents want to hear, especially about the other parent, and will often deny themselves things in their own life in order to please the parent they are with. Following the breakup of their parents, they have learned that love is a "conditional" entity, which though once there, can be taken or lost without reason or explanation. They will do anything not to have that happen to them. Children perceive things, and those perceptions become the child's reality.

Parents must know that they have an extra duty to their children following separation and divorce: to help bring stability and continuity to children who have otherwise lost their "normal" life pattern. Even though parents may no longer be marriage partners, they will always be parent partners. This will not be easy. The process of working with a former spouse— who may have betrayed; or a spouse who was once loved and trusted, but because of their actions destroyed that trust, causing the loss of a loving relationship—will be very difficult. Sometimes, it is almost impossible. But children of divorce are part of both parents and deserve the right to love both parents without fear of retaliation from one parent because they love the other parent, too.

Think about it. If a child has two friends who they really like, but they perceive those two friends not liking each other, how do they choose between their two friends? Are they not torn when they want to have a party or do something and would like to have both their friends with them? Multiply that agony thousands of times, and that is how children of divorce feel when they think or perceive the two people who are the closest to them in their life—their mom and dad—not liking each other. How do they choose? And, as the adults who made the decision to divorce, should you force your child to be put in the middle to have to make such an impossible decision?

The greatest gift parents of divorce can give their children is the right and the freedom to love their other parent. They will love them regardless of what you choose. But when you are part of the process of allowing them that right to have those feelings, as opposed to forcing them to hide them from you, you open a door to your children, which allows them to know they are secure with you and that they can share their feelings with you.

Children learn not from what they are told but from what they see, feel, and experience. If a parent is worried that they must "compete" with the other parent when bad-mouthing occurs, and if they do not answer "in kind," their child may believe what is said about them by the other parent, they should know that the truth of who and what they are will be known by their child, not from what may be told about them by an angry or bitter person, but rather on whether their child feels love, trust, and respect for them. Those are the feelings that last a lifetime. Those are what parents of divorce should strive to earn from their children. But to earn love, trust, and respect, adult decisions will require adult responsibilities. These responsibilities may sometimes seem like unfair burdens or benefits to an undeserving other parent. But you are not doing it for that other parent; you are doing it for your child. In fact, you are also doing it for yourself.

From Attorney:
MIRIAM Z. WOLOCK, J.D.

Hickey, Cianciolo, Fishman & Finn
901 Wilshire Drive, Suite 400
Troy, MI 48084
p: (248) 247-3300 | **e:** mwolock@wolocklaw.com
w: www.hclawyers.com

Winning and losing are concepts that apply to sports and elections, but not families. When my clients start "keeping score" (Who has more days? Who has more vacation time? Who has more toys at their place?), we sit down and talk frankly about the conceptual framework of two-parent households. I call this a parenting partnership. The parenting partnership replaces the marital partnership that ended with divorce.

No one wins or loses in a parenting partnership. Like any successful partners, if you think of yourself and your former spouse as "in the same boat," your partnership will succeed. Your shared goals are the emotional and physical well-being of your children. You have to work together so that the parenting partnership, and ultimately the children, thrive and prosper.

Is this easy? Of course not. Even the best partners have disagreements. And this partnership has changed to a post-marital relationship. But if you insist on winning, the post-divorce partnership will never take root, and you and your children will suffer for it.

CHAPTER 3

HAVING CONVERSATIONS WITHOUT FIGHTING

I'm right, and you're wrong!

Sound familiar? How many times have you said those words out loud to your former spouse or in your head as you feel you are about to explode?

What Makes Parenting Conversations Difficult?

- When the other parent accuses or blames you.
- When you're caught off guard and the other parent brings up a topic you are not prepared to discuss.
- When you don't ever want to talk about the subject raised by the other parent.
- When the other parent starts a conversation in front of the children or other people that should remain just between the two of you.
- When you feel badgered or bullied.
- When you are disrespected or undermined.
- When you are held hostage by the other parent's threats to take action against you or your children.

Hard as it may be to accept, you and your former spouse are partners in parenting and will be connected through your children forever, and you need to make that partnership work for the sake of your children. There will be many times throughout the years that you disagree when making decisions. I can imagine there might be certain topics you need to discuss, but just thinking about the impending conversation makes you anxious. You and your former spouse likely had communication problems when you were married. Resorting to old ways of talking is probably not a good idea, especially if there are still hard feelings between you. Yet you must find a way to resolve dilemmas related to your children.

The $64 million question: How can you turn difficult conversations into productive ones when you want to talk about a sensitive subject?

Start the Difficult Conversation

Simply ask for the conversation. Tell your former spouse that you want to talk about something. Give him or her the courtesy of choosing the right time to talk. State the reason or purpose for the conversation:

I'd like to talk with you about how we might handle the costs of the kids' summer activities. Is this a good time for you, or would you rather talk at a different time?

Find Out What Your Former Spouse is Thinking and Feeling

It is risky to assume that you know what the other person is thinking and feeling. You cannot read your former spouse's mind and you would not appreciate it if he/she attempted to read yours. Approach this task respectfully by initiating, for instance:

I'm wondering if you've given any thought to how we can pay for the kids' summer activities. Maybe you'd like to tell me what you're feeling about this.

Reflect What You Have Just Heard

Keep an open mind and try not to let prior experiences cloud the current interaction. You may be surprised by what you hear. Then, before you offer your opinions, rephrase what you heard so your former spouse knows you are listening, and restate how you think he or she feels about what was just said. Example:

Former Spouse: *My hours got cut back at work for the summer, and I'm not making as much as when I originally said I would pay for the kids' swimming lessons and day camp.*

You: *So, you're saying your funds are unexpectedly tight right now. You must be disappointed that you have to reconsider the ways you can contribute to the kids' summer plans.*

Invite the Other Person to Hear Your Points of View

Once your former spouse realizes you are willing to listen to what he or she has to say, you are more likely to engage in an open dialogue. Now simply ask him or her to listen to you. Example:

Would you be interested in hearing my thoughts on this?

Identify the Points of Agreement

When you are engaged in a difficult conversation about the children, consider making a statement that reminds you and your former spouse that you are a partnership working for the children and that you both have their best interests at heart. For instance:

You: *I believe when we made our first agreement about financing the kids' summer activities, we were both thinking it would be best to keep them busy this summer so they wouldn't sit in front of the television or be on the computer all day.*

Exchange Suggestions

Don't come on too strongly. Try an easy-to-hear suggestion that invites your former spouse to the talking table. Example:

Money is tight for me right now, too. Maybe we can think of some alternatives that would be less expensive for both of us and would still give the kids some structured time this summer. What do you think?

When Ideas Clash, Ask for a Compromise

Some conversations start smoothly enough and then hit the wall. At some point, you may find yourself butting heads over two different plans. Now what? Ask for a compromise. For example:

You: *It seems we don't exactly agree on an alternative plan. You want the kids to go to the free day camp at the park, and while I like the activities that are listed in the brochure, I don't think there's enough adult supervision for the number of young children they intend to enroll. I really wanted to send them to Dolly's Day Camp five days a week.*

Former Spouse: *Well we don't have enough money for Dolly's Day Camp.*

You: *You're right about that. Maybe we can combine our ideas. You are suggesting that we find someplace free to send them, and I really wanted to send them to Dolly's. My parents had offered to take them two or three days a week. Would you be willing to consider enrolling them in Dolly's Day Camp for part of the week?*

Former Spouse: *I think we can afford that a lot easier, and if I get more hours later this summer, we can maybe send them one more day to Dolly's.*

Remember: Talk to the other parent the way you want him or her to talk to you. Be willing to listen. Give up the need to be right or to make the other person wrong. Make a commitment to resolve differences peacefully for the sake of providing a conflict-free zone for your children. Don't they deserve that much from you?

CHAPTER 4

FAMILIAR CONVERSATIONS

This chapter contains vignettes about the most frequently reported hot topics. You will read two conversations about each topic. The first will be an all-too-familiar contentious failure. The second will be a preferred approach to the same topic. You may find yourself drowning in one or more of these scenarios. Stay positive! Help is here! Try some of these alternative methods and reinforce your co-parenting partnership. It's a lot more satisfying and enjoyable when parenting partners communicate well and are able to model problem-solving for your children.

Difficult Conversations ...

About Money

Abby: *Bobby's marching band is going to the national competition in Washington, D.C. He needs $600.*

Alan: *So, what do you want from me? I'm not paying for that. I just spent $55 on new basketball shoes for him.*

Abby: *You make plenty of money. You've already taken two vacations this year. If you can go to Europe for two weeks and take a Caribbean cruise, you can certainly support your son in something important for his school.*

Alan: *Nobody ever helped me when I was a kid. My parents made me pay for everything, and I turned out OK. He can get a job and pay his own way.*

Abby: *He doesn't have time for a job. Between school,*

basketball, and band, he barely has time for his homework, and you're always riding him about his grades. Besides, the trip is in four weeks, and he could never earn the money by then. Who would hire him anyway? He's only fourteen.

Alan: *You're always coddling him. I'm not stopping you from helping him; you pay it!*

Abby: *I knew we couldn't count on you, Alan. You were never generous when we were married. Why should I suddenly expect you would be different now?*

Abby and Alan are having a battle full of blame and accusations, slinging declarations of disappointment and disapproval. Abby knew going into the conversation that asking for Alan's financial help for Bobby would be a hot button because of Alan's resentment toward his own parents for refusing to support him while he was growing up.

Let's see how this same scenario could be handled more satisfactorily:

Abby: *Alan, when you have some time, I'd like to talk with you about Bobby's marching band.*

Alan: *I'm free now. What's up?*

Abby: *Bobby's band qualified for the national competition in Washington, D.C., next month. The school wants the families to participate in the cost of sending the students.*

Alan: *What does that mean?*

Abby: *Bobby has to come up with $600 to be able to go. I'm wondering if you and I can talk about how we might help Bobby raise the money for his trip.*

Alan: *Well, I just spent $55 on basketball shoes for him. He should earn his own money for the trip. My parents didn't help me; why should I help him? He'll never learn any responsibility.*

Abby: *It sounds like you would feel resentful having to contribute money toward the trip.*

Alan: *Yeah. It never stops. This month Washington, next month he'll need money for another pair of basketball shoes because his feet start growing as soon as we walk out of the store.*

Abby: *Raising a child is expensive, isn't it?*

Alan: *It's not as if I don't have the money. I don't think we should just hand over money every time the kid needs something extra.*

Abby: *It sounds like you think Bobby should take some responsibility for this trip. I need to pay more attention to that. Do you think we could put our heads together and figure this thing out?*

Alan: *OK. Go on.*

Abby: *I appreciate your suggestion that Bobby participate in making this trip happen; I have to admit that I would have just handed over the money, but I agree with you that he will learn responsibility for himself if he has to earn his way. I'm glad you spoke up because I tend to coddle him, and I need to let him grow up and become more responsible.*

Alan: *For a change you are listening to me! So what are you proposing?*

Abby: *The trip is only four weeks away and I don't think it's realistic for Bobby to earn the entire $600 by then since his time is so limited and he's only fourteen. Would you be willing to talk about a plan to help him get the money while he's learning responsibility at the same time?*

Alan: *That's better than just forking over the money. Why don't we split it three ways? We'll each give him $200 and he has to earn the other $200 in four weeks and that's just $50 a week. He could earn that by cutting our lawns and cleaning our basements and garages.*

Abby: *Alan, I like the way you think! Let's talk to him together when I drop him off at your house later.*

About Parenting Styles

(Censoring, movies, music, dress codes, language, exposure to older kids, eating habits, bedtime)

Bella: *I'm sick of having this conversation. How many times have I told you that my kids aren't allowed to see movies rated above PG and they can't listen to rap because I don't want them hearing those words. They're already learning to swear, and you let them swear in your house.*

Barry: *They're not your kids; they're our kids, and I can do whatever I want when they're with me. I don't believe in censoring. They're going to see and hear things, and I'd rather they do it with me when I can explain ...*

Bella: *The other thing I've told you a million times is not to let them hang out with older kids.*

Barry: *They need to learn street smarts. You can't be with them all the time. How are they going to know what to do?*

Bella: *They're way too young! And you let Molly wear clothes that are too tight and too low-cut. What are you trying to do? She's only twelve, and you're letting her look like she's twenty! High school guys are hitting on her.*

Barry: *You're overreacting. She just wants to look like the other girls in her class. You were always such a prude.*

Bella: *You have no idea how to be a parent. Who lets their kids eat cold pizza for breakfast? You let the kids eat whatever they want. How are they going to learn healthy eating habits that way?*

Barry: *Kids eat what they need. And don't start complaining that they don't get enough sleep. I let them decide that for themselves. When they're tired, they go to sleep. They hate it when you make them go to bed by 8:30 even if they're not tired. You're so rigid!*

Bella: *You just don't want to do the hard work that it takes to raise children. You always make me look like the bad guy; you never support me.*

Barry: *All you do is complain about me. I can never do anything right. And you wonder why I divorced you?*

Bella and Barry have very different parenting styles. Barry is more nonchalant in his approach, while Bella has a more structured and controlled approach to parenting. Issues like censoring movies, language, dress code, proper eating habits, and bedtimes are all hot buttons. How can these two parents have productive conversations about their children when they fundamentally disagree?

Let's look at a different kind of conversation where both can express their viewpoints and make some decisions that work for both of them:

Bella: *Barry, there are a few things about the kids I want to talk with you about. Let me know when you have about half an hour to talk.*

Barry: *How 'bout now? The kids are in the other room watching a DVD. I don't think they can hear us.*

Bella: *Last week, I was talking to my sister about some guy from work who asked me out, and I didn't think the kids were listening and later they asked me who I was going out with. Those kids have ears everywhere. I would be more comfortable if we could maybe go outside while we're talking.*

Barry: *OK. (Pause) What do you want to talk about?*

Bella: *I'm concerned about some of the choices the kids are making lately, and I'm trying to decide if they are just mimicking something they are seeing on television or if they are beginning to experiment with risky behavior.*

Barry: *Like what? What are you talking about?*

Bella: *Molly has been strutting around in very low-cut tops, and her jeans are barely covering her privates. How do you feel about high school boys hitting on her?*

Barry: *I remember what I was like in high school and … yeah … not good. But that's what she chooses to wear, and I wouldn't know what to say to her without sounding like I'm looking at her, too.*

Bella: *I imagine it's a lot harder for a father to talk about those things with a daughter than a son. If I have that talk with her, would you be willing to back me on it?*

Barry: *OK. But what do I say when she starts arguing with me just as she's leaving the house and she's late?*

Bella: *I have no problem if you want to put this on me. You can tell her it's my rule and you're backing me up, or you can tell her this is something we decided together, although she will probably think it came from me anyway.*

Barry: *I don't want to look like a wimp. I'll tell her it was our decision together and she won't try to play one of us against the other.*

Bella: *I don't know where she gets these ideas. Do you?*

Barry: *She watches programs and goes to the movies and sees everything.*

Bella: *How do you feel about limiting what she watches?*

Barry: *I don't know. I never really paid that much attention before, but lately, it's getting out of hand.*

Bella: *Yeah, I know what you mean. Well, they're our children and I'm wondering if you would be willing to think of some ways we can address these issues before we lose our strength with them.*

Barry: *So, OK … I guess …*

Bella: *How would you feel about limiting their television and movies to G and PG?*

Barry: *If we're both doing the same thing, I could do that.*

Bella: *Also, do you think our language is setting a good example for them? The younger ones are getting kind of mouthy.*

Barry: *We both swear way too much in front of them.*

Bella: *Barry, I'm really glad we can talk like this about the kids, because I know we both love them and want to be good parents. I also know we don't always agree on things, and I never want to appear like I'm controlling what goes on in your house like what they eat and what time they go to bed.*

Barry: *I don't really care about the food. Kids eat what they need. Same as sleep. They go to bed when they need to.*

Bella: *Since we changed the parenting time plan and we each have them half of each week, I've noticed some changes in them. Would you be willing to monitor them and see if they seem more tired than normal? Sometimes I wonder if the younger ones just want to be like Molly and try to stay up late even when they're tired.*

Barry: *That's a good point. OK, I'll watch it. And I'll try to give them better meals.*

Bella: *It's hard raising kids and working full time. I know the kids appreciate all our efforts, and I appreciate yours!*

About Values and Attitudes

(Religion, children's activities, talking in front of the children, children's vs. parents' needs)

Carl: *I told you before; you have to get them up early Sunday mornings in order to get them to church on time when you have them for the weekend.*

Cara: *I work all week, and I just want to sleep in on Sundays. It's bad enough that I have to drive them to Scouts after school and the library after dinner ... when do I have time for anything for myself?*

Carl: *Your attitude stinks! Nothing ever changes with you. You just think of yourself and when you will be free to see your boyfriend. Meanwhile, every kid in school is involved in after-school activities, but you're too lazy to get them involved.*

Cara: *Screw you!*

Carl: *Well, that's just great. And by the way, you could watch your mouth in front of the kids. They're picking up on your nasty attitude, and they have no respect for authority anymore.*

Cara: *This is clearly why I divorced you! This conversation is over!*

Carl raises some important parenting issues with his former spouse; however, she is completely unwilling to discuss his concerns because he has distracted her from the issues with accusations and blame. How can Carl improve his approach?

Carl: *Hi Cara. Do you have time to talk about a couple of things regarding the kids?*

Cara: *You know I don't have much time. You can see how busy I am trying to hold down a job and drive the kids everywhere. There's never enough time just for me.*

Carl: *You mentioned this before, and I know how hard it is to raise kids and try to manage your own life, too. I'm sure we are both doing the best we can. Actually, that is what I wanted to talk with you about. Is now a good time?*

Cara: *Why not?*

Carl: *You and I had agreed that the children would go to church on Sundays, and whoever had them would make sure they got there. Is this still a priority with you?*

Cara: *I do want them to go, but I can't seem to get moving on Sunday mornings. By the end of the weekend, I'm collapsing.*

Carl: *Maybe together we can think of a different way to get them to church. Would you be willing to talk about that?*

Cara: *You would actually help me?*

Carl: *We'd both be helping our children get what we both want them to have. That goes for the after-school programs, too. We both want them involved and don't want them to be left out.*

Cara: *Do you have any ideas?*

Carl: *One idea is to have them go to church with their cousins. They only live two blocks away, and my sister could swing by and pick them up. Would you be willing to have them ready?*

Cara: *That's really great! Yes, thank you. I'll have them ready, and then I can go back to bed. Maybe I could ask my friend Mary if she could drive them home from soccer after school. If she could, I will sign them up.*

Carl: *I like that plan. Then the kids won't miss anything their friends are doing. Is there something I can help you with?*

Cara: *I can't think of anything right now, but I appreciate that you understand where I'm coming from.*

Carl: *Well, I appreciate we're able to talk like this for the benefit of our kids. I have one more thought: Maybe we could talk like this in front of the kids so they can see us being respectful to each other.*

Cara: *That would be better for them, wouldn't it?*

About Responsibilities
(Timeliness, communication, organization, transferring children's belongings)

David: *How many times do I have to tell you not to be late! Jeffrey sits in the front window waiting for you, and he worries that you either forgot him or something bad has happened to you. He's only four years old, and he doesn't understand your pedicure was running over.*

Darla: *Can't you relax? You are so anal, Type A! If you would just chill, Jeffrey would, too.*

David: *You do this with everything. You make Jeffrey late for swim class, you forget to tell me when his doctors' appointments are, and then it's too late for me to rearrange my calendar. You're so unorganized that you don't send all his stuff back to my house.*

Darla: *Stop yelling at me! You're not my father!*

By the time their exchange of insults ended, David had forgotten what he wanted to say to Darla. Nothing was accomplished. Let's see how he could have helped Darla join him in his concerns about parental responsibilities:

David: *Darla, I was hoping we could have a few minutes to talk. Is this a good time?*

Darla: *I don't want to get into another fighting match, so if you're going to criticize me, I'm not interested.*

David: *I can understand why you would think that. I probably come on too strong when I want to talk about Jeffrey. I have to remember that you love him as much as I do and we both want to be good parents to him.*

Darla: *So, what do you want to talk about?*

David: *Have you noticed that when Jeffrey is waiting for me to pick him up from your house, he becomes anxious?*

Darla: *Now that you mention it, yes.*

David: *I think he may worry that he has been forgotten or that something awful has happened to one of us.*

Darla: *Aw! Poor little guy. I never thought about it from his point of view.*

David: *Maybe we should be more conscious of getting to each other's house on time so he doesn't get anxious. Are there some other times when he gets anxious that you can think of?*

Darla: *Well, he might be when I'm running late getting him to swim class.*

David: *I'm thinking he might be anxious when I don't show up for his doctors' appointments. Maybe he thinks I don't care or forgot.*

Darla: *I honestly never thought about that.*

David: *I've also noticed how anxious he becomes when he has forgotten something at one of our houses.*

Darla: *That happens a lot. Oh, I feel terrible for him!*

David: *What can we do to avoid putting him in these situations?*

Darla: *I have a new neighbor who is divorced, and he and his ex-wife use an online family calendar so nobody forgets the important stuff.*

David: *Could you find out more about that? It sounds good. We could try it. What can we do to remind ourselves to send Jeffrey's clothes and toys back and forth between our houses?*

Darla: *Maybe we can find some ideas online for that, too. Could you look into that since I'm going to research the family calendar?*

David: *Sure. I'll get back to you, and I just want to say how much I appreciate that we can talk about these things.*

About School

Effie: *You promised me the children could go to private schools. Why are you backing out now? Is your new wife resentful about the money you are spending on your children? You never had any backbone.*

Ezra: *I just told you why I can't send them; you never listen to anything I have to say. You're living in a fantasy world.*

Effie and Ezra are doing a familiar dance that is reminiscent of battles they fought during their marriage. Effie wants to club Ezra over the head with guilt and taunt him with threats on his manliness. Ezra can't wait for the bickering to end and loses awareness of the issue at hand. How can Effie talk to Ezra about private schools in a more satisfactory way?

Effie: *Ezra, let me know when you have a few minutes to talk about where the children will be going to school next fall.*

Ezra: *We can talk now. I know you want to send them to private school, and that's something we both actually want. But I am having some problems, and I don't think I can swing it financially.*

Effie: *What has changed since we made the agreement to send them to private school?*

Ezra: *I know it may look like my new wife is against the expenditure, but she is actually willing to contribute part* of her income to our kids' tuition because she graduated from private school and believes in it.

Effie: *Wow, that's amazing. I never could have imagined that! So what's the problem?*

Ezra: *I was just notified that I'm getting a drastic pay cut and my entire job may be in jeopardy.*

Effie: *Oh, I'm so sorry. I had no idea. Now I understand why you have been reluctant to talk about this. Would you be open to brainstorming some ideas together to try to send the children to private school?*

Ezra: *Yes. I really want to send them, but I couldn't see how it's possible under these circumstances.*

Effie: *Would you be willing to make a confidential appointment to see the financial aid director at the school to appeal our case? We can go together.*

Ezra: *That sounds like a good place to start. I appreciate your tolerance right now, and I'll try everything I can to keep my promise.*

About What Children Report

Fred: *Why are you running out of money? You're getting enough alimony to keep you in your Mercedes, and you get enough child support to feed half the neighborhood.*

Fran: *What are you talking about? I'm sick of you harping on me about money!*

Fred: *Carrie told me you ran out of money for groceries last week.*

Fran: *Why don't you just ask me about things instead of assuming that everything the kids tell you is true? You never cared about my side of the story; why should you care now?*

Fred and Fran are having a spat about a common problem among divorced families. Children tend to report what they see and hear in one house to the parent in the other house. The parents often jump to wrong conclusions instead of doing a reality check in an adult conversation. What might that look like?

Fred: *Carrie told me you ran out of money for groceries. I was suspicious of her perceptions, so I thought we could talk and figure out what she might have misperceived.*

Fran: *I really appreciate you coming to me before jumping to the wrong conclusion. Here's the real story: I took the kids apple-picking this weekend. I thought it would be a great family outing and would get them out in the fresh fall air. We had a great time. Later that night, I overheard Carrie telling one of her friends that we don't have much money since the divorce so now we have to pick our own food.*

Fred: *Wow! Am I glad I talked to you!*

About Relocation

Gary: *I'm moving to California, and I want the kids on holidays and during the summers.*

Gail: *I knew I could never count on you. You promised we would be married forever and you dumped me for a younger wife. Now you want to move out of state. Are you kidding me? I shouldn't have to be punished by giving up my vacations and summers with the kids just because you now have a new plan for your new life!*

Gary: *You have them all the time. I'm their father and I get to see them, too. I figured you wouldn't understand. You just want to hoard them and you're jealous of my wife. I'll see you back in court!*

Gail and Gary have a new challenge: how to re-address the parenting time plan to accommodate the children's need to see their father after he moves to California. Their unwillingness to empathize with each other's position becomes an impediment in their ability to solve the issue. How can they have a productive conversation when feelings are so raw?

Gary: *Gail, there is something really difficult I need to talk with you about. Are you free now to talk?*

Gail: *Sounds serious. What's wrong?*

Gary: *I know how devastating the divorce was for you; it was sad for me, too. And it must seem like I have had an easier time moving on with my life than you have. My family and friends have dropped me since I married Wendy. I'm having a really hard time adjusting and sometimes I wish this whole thing never happened. Being out of work hasn't helped. I feel like I've let the family down again. Anyway, I got an amazing job offer in California, and I've decided to take it. Wendy and I will be moving in a month. I'm going to need to re-look at the parenting time plan to see how I can see the kids.*

Gail: *I hope you don't think you are going to completely upset my life again!*

Gary: *Actually, that's why I want to have this conversation with you. I thought if we could talk about this together, we could work something out that would let the kids have time with their father and not be too big of a problem for you.*

Gail: *I'm not exactly thrilled with this idea, but maybe with you in California, the weekly routine with the kids would be simpler and less chaotic. What do you have in mind for a schedule?*

Gary: *I'd like to work something out so you don't have to be without the kids for some holidays and summer times, just like we have it now. Maybe we can start with our current plan and tweak it a bit. Are you open for trying?*

Gail: *That sounds better than going to court.*

About Dating

Hank: *I don't want you parading your dates in front of my kids!*

Heidi: *Well, you don't have much to say about it, do you? They're my kids, too, and I'll do whatever I want!*

Dating after a marriage ends is a sensitive topic. Hank's request has a lot of emotion behind it, but Heidi can only hear his demands and isn't the least bit motivated to talk productively. Let's see how their conversation can improve:

Hank: *You seem to have started dating, Heidi. I was wondering if you have some time when we could talk about the kids' reactions to both of us as we begin to start our new lives.*

Heidi: *You're not going to start telling me what to do, are you?*

Hank: *I was hoping we could talk about the kids and their feelings, perceptions, and reactions to our choices.*

Heidi: *Well, I guess so.*

Hank: *What do you think the kids might be thinking and feeling when you and I introduce them to people we are dating?*

Heidi: *That they're just new friends of ours.*

Hank: *You know, I thought the same thing. In fact, last week I went out with a woman I've seen a few times, and I wanted to show off the kids to her. It was very innocent. I'm not serious with this woman. Well anyway, it was a big mistake. Katie was rude to her and the next day yelled at me for being disloyal to you. She said I wasn't thinking of her feelings. She said my dating was embarrassing her in front of her friends and she didn't want another mother. I told her the woman was just a friend and she said to me, "Do you think I'm stupid?"*

Heidi: *Oh man, I had no idea! Should we talk to them and tell them dating doesn't mean anything?*

Hank: *That's an idea, but Katie is starting to date, and she might take that to mean what she is doing is insignificant.*

Heidi: *You got a point there. Do you have any ideas?*

Hank: *Does it make sense to you that maybe we both limit our dating to non-parenting times and introduce dates to the kids only once a relationship becomes serious?*

Heidi: *I agree that we shouldn't introduce anyone to them until something becomes serious, but limiting my social life to non-parenting times isn't going to work for me. I feel like you're trying to control my life a little here!*

Hank: *I understand how you could feel that way because I'm talking about what goes on in your life, and we no longer share that life. Frankly, my main concern is not exposing the kids to random people, and I appreciate your willingness to talk about this.*

Heidi: *OK, let's agree that from now on, we won't introduce people we are just dating to the kids until a relationship becomes serious. If I have a date during my parenting time, I will plan to meet him somewhere instead of having him pick me up at the house.*

Hank: *That sounds like a plan. I'm very glad we can have conversations like this so that we can talk about what's best for our kids. I know we both love them and want to be good parents. Thanks, Heidi.*

About New Spouses

Ida: *She's a witch, and I'm not sending our ten-year-old daughter to your house until you can get your wife under control!*

Irv: *My wife does everything for that ungrateful child. She acts like a brat to her because you're poisoning her mind.*

Ida: *Sally's afraid of her, and I'm not going to stand by while you do nothing. Sally's having nightmares and doesn't want to go to your house anymore.*

Irv: *Sally's going to have to learn to fight her own battles. And you stay the hell out of it!*

This conversation between Ida and Irv didn't help Sally at all, and it sure didn't promote a good co-parenting relationship. Ida's concern for Sally's comfort is legitimate, but Irv could only hear Ida's attack on his new wife. Enraged, he couldn't focus on the issue. How could this conversation improve and end with a better outcome for Sally?

Ida: *Irv, do you have a few minutes to talk about Sally?*

Irv: *Yes, this is a good time. What do you have on your mind?*

Ida: *Does Sally seem agitated when she goes to your house lately?*

Irv: *I don't know if I'd call it agitated. She's sarcastic and unreasonable! She and my wife are at it lately, and my wife thinks she's an ungrateful little brat.*

Ida: *That must be very uncomfortable for you being in the middle.*

Irv: *It is! Not having any children of her own, my wife expects Sally to be perfect. I keep telling her that kids are wrapped up in their own worlds and aren't perfect.*

Ida: *It must be difficult to try to please them both. Do*

you think Sally wants to avoid going to your house because she doesn't know how to manage the situation?

Irv: *Well, that's possible; after all, she's just a kid.*

Ida: *It may seem like I am poisoning her against your wife, but I want you to know that I don't want Sally growing up running away from problems. I've been encouraging her to go over there. Can you and I talk about some ways we can help Sally cope?*

Irv: *I'm grateful for the conversation. I'm at the end of my rope here, and I don't want another divorce on my hands. When I try talking to my wife, she accuses me of taking sides against her.*

Ida: *I'm so sorry you are having to go through this. I can't offer much help about your wife, but I was thinking about Sally. Do you think spending time alone with Sally might ease some of the tension?*

Irv: *Now that you mention it, I think part of the problem is that Sally feels like I replaced her. I'll talk to my wife about this idea. I think she'll actually be relieved that she doesn't have to deal with Sally all weekend. Sometimes she acts like a resentful babysitter.*

Ida: *I'm glad we had this talk. We always do well when we think about Sally's best interests.*

CHAPTER 5

SUMMARY AND TAKEAWAYS

When divorce happens for couples with children, the marriage may be over, but a co-parenting relationship needs to continue, leaving open the potential for future disputes.

There are two common occurrences in divorce and post-divorce arguments that become roadblocks to reaching agreements: unresolved feelings and poor communication techniques.

01. Unresolved Feelings

It's never about the money! People often fight about one thing when, in actuality, they are harboring feelings about something completely different. For instance, when one parent argues that his former spouse is not paying enough child support, he may really want to reveal his underlying feeling that his former spouse should pay restitution to him because he was devastated when she filed for the divorce against his will.

Unresolved issues from the past and harbored feelings that may have been swept under the carpet have a way of intruding on conversations about current issues. This becomes evident when one person begins to talk and is suddenly surprised by the other person's reaction.

02. Poor Communication Techniques

Anticipating a difficult conversation with your former spouse can really make you squirm. You think about what you're going to say and how your former spouse is going to explode. You can predict how it will go because you have had variations of this conversation many times before. You may even find yourself yelling in your opening statement just so you will have a running start, or to emphasize your concern. The conclusion is rarely satisfying to either, you are left with the same unresolved issues, and you are back in court!

A family can find happiness and peace after divorce, but it cannot build a positive future on top of a battleground. The fighting must stop!

The most important reason to stop fighting is to provide a conflict-free zone for your children.

Children need to be able to grow up unfettered by the complications of adult relationships. They need to be free of worry that they have done something to cause the strife between their parents.

A dispute resolution clause is often absent from the written divorce settlement, so once the divorce is over you have no roadmap to guide you through your arguments. Without a plan, your smallest spats can become full-blown battles. This never promotes a good co-parenting relationship and is absolutely destructive for everyone in the family.

Dispute resolution requires the willingness of you and your former spouse to engage in negotiations about touchy topics until you come to a conclusion with which you can both live. The conclusions may not be ideal for either of you, but they must be workable and durable.

Following are a few methods of resolving post-divorce disputes:

- The most extreme measure of dispute resolution between co-parents is to appear before the court. This is the least preferable option because the judge does not know the intricacies of your family and may intervene in ways less acceptable to both of you. It is also costly and contentious and does not promote the confidence, motivation, nor the feelings of success needed for conflict resolution on future issues.

- A parenting coordinator is sometimes appointed by the court either through the Friend of the Court or by agreement of the parties to help resolve conflicts and encourage positive decision-making.

- Each judge has at least one referee and a Friend of the Court counselor assigned to him or her. Sometimes the judge may ask the referee to settle disputes between co-parents.

- Friend of the Court counselors are employed by the county. Parties can call the Friend of the Court counselor directly to assist in conflict resolution.

- If your divorce settlement has a post-divorce dispute resolution clause, you may choose to exercise that plan. The clause usually names a neutral professional whom you, your former spouse, and your attorneys agreed at the finalization of the divorce would be the "go-to" person if you hit a post-divorce snag. Your neutral "go-to" may be a therapist, counselor, mediator, or divorce coach. Use your resources before you allow your co-parenting relationship to deteriorate.

- In the end, it is always advisable to talk between yourselves. Express your ideas and listen to each other. Look for common ground. You may actually devise a compromise that works for both of you and is in the best interests of your family. If you are able to resolve your conflicts together without assistance, your successes will become building blocks for future experiences. Use the principles you have read in this book to help you have more productive conversations.

Takeaways:

Have a Productive Conversation
- To start, ask the other person for a good time to talk.
- State your purpose.
- Discover what the other person is thinking and feeling.
- Reflect what you have heard to the other person.
- Invite the other person to hear your points of view.
- Identify points of agreement.
- Exchange suggestions.
- When ideas clash, ask for compromise.
- If you reach an impasse, agree on a neutral third party.
- It is highly advisable that a dispute resolution plan be in place for the times when you just cannot agree and all attempts at those difficult conversations fail.

Remember: Talk to your parenting partner the way you want him or her to talk to you. Be willing to listen. Give up the need to be right or to make the other person wrong. Make a commitment to resolve differences peacefully for the sake of providing a conflict-free zone for your children. They deserve it!

Suggestions:

- Do not accuse or blame.
- When you are caught off guard or not prepared for the conversation, ask the person for another time to talk.
- Do not talk about adult issues in front of the children.
- Do not bully or badger the other parent into an agreement.
- Do not use the children to threaten the other parent into agreement.
- Beware of the continuation of domestic abuse post-divorce. If you feel at risk, notify the police and your attorney, and seek professional help.

Remember: The importance of "family" is always magnified and accentuated for children of divorce. Children tend to blame themselves for whatever goes wrong between parents. No family's life is perfect. Disagreements will arise. If you do not demonstrate civility when resolving disputes, your children will blame themselves! In order to thrive, they need to see their parents joining forces as successful co-parents devoted to the family. Be good role models for your children. Show them that conflict is not frightening and can be overcome with reason and respect. Your personal feelings are not as important as your children's needs.

ABOUT THE AUTHOR

 **Dr. Nancy Fishman** is a psychologist and author in private practice in Birmingham, Michigan. She received her doctorate from Wayne State University in 1979 and has since been certified in Divorce Mediation and Collaborative Law. She has trained at Harvard University Law School in Advanced Negotiations. She specializes in areas related to the family, including marriage, divorce, and life after divorce. She also conducts business and divorce mediations, serves as a parenting coordinator, conducts custody evaluations, and provides expert testimony on family-related issues.

Dr. Fishman is a co-collaborator of the international program, SMILE: Start Making It Liveable for Everyone. She is also the founder of Forgotten Harvest, soon to be the nation's largest fresh food rescue operation.

She and her husband survived raising three children together and now live in Birmingham, Michigan.

You may visit her websites at:
www.NancyFishmanPhD.com &
www.TheFamilyLawDoctor.com

Photo by Natalie Probst